Bees

Aaron Frisch

CREATIVE EDUCATION • CREATIVE PAPERBACKS

seedlings

Published by Creative Education and Creative Paperbacks
P.O. Box 227, Mankato, Minnesota 56002
Creative Education and Creative Paperbacks are
imprints of The Creative Company
www.thecreativecompany.us

Design and production by Ellen Huber
Art direction by Rita Marshall
Printed in the United States of America

Photographs by Alamy (WILDLIFE GmbH), Corbis (Fritz
Rauschenbach), Dreamstime (PeterWaters, Stockfotocz),
Getty Images (Ingo Arndt, Heidi & Hans-Jurgen Koch,
Thomas Lottermoser, Visuals Unlimited, Inc./Eric Tourneret),
Shutterstock (12_Tribes, Alekcey, Geanina Bechea, irin-k,
kesipun, Jun Mu, PCHT, sergey23, Craig Taylor, Peter Waters),
SuperStock (Minden Pictures)

Library of Congress Cataloging-in-Publication Data
Frisch, Aaron.
Bees / Aaron Frisch.
p. cm. — (Seedlings)
Includes bibliographical references and index.
Summary: A kindergarten-level introduction to bees, covering
their growth process, behaviors, the hives they call home, and
such defining physical features as their stingers.
ISBN 978-1-60818-456-9 (hardcover)
ISBN 978-1-62832-038-1 (pbk)
1. Bees—Juvenile literature. I. Title.

QL568.A6F598 2014
595.79'9—dc23   2013029062

CCSS: RI.K.1, 2, 3, 4, 5, 6, 7;
RI.1.1, 2, 3, 4, 5, 6, 7; RF.K.1, 3; RF.1.1

HC 9 8 7 6 5 4
PBK 11 10 9

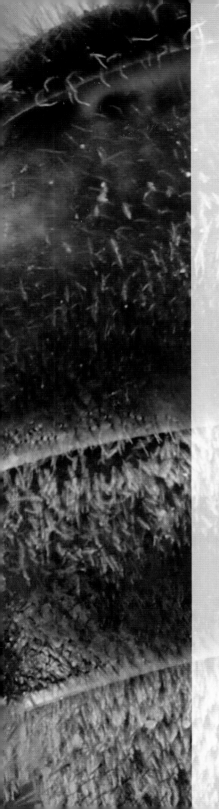
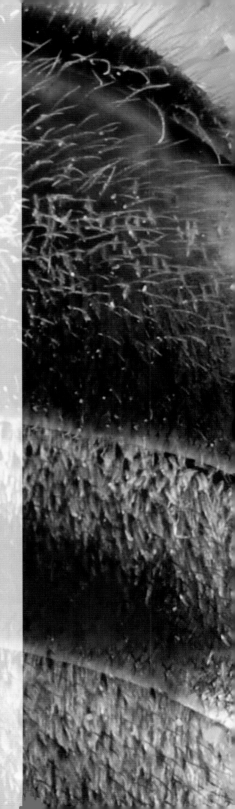

TABLE OF CONTENTS

Hello, bees!

Bees are bugs that fly.

They make a buzzing sound.

Bees have striped bodies. They have two pairs of wings. Some bees have sharp stingers.

Bees live in big groups.
They build nests in trees or rocks.

A bee nest is
called a hive.

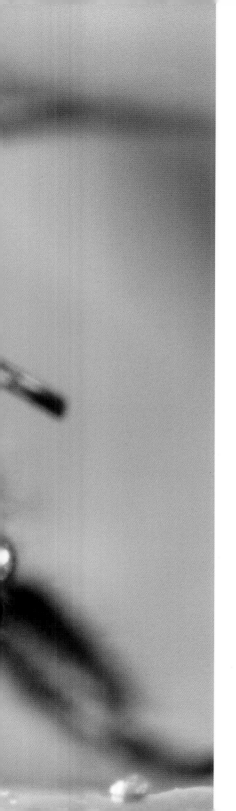

Bees pick up pollen and nectar from flowers. They make nectar into honey.

A baby bee comes out of an egg. First it looks like a worm.

But it grows quickly!

Bees fly around to find food. They keep the hive clean. They feed baby bees.

Goodbye, bees!

Picture a Bee

mouth

eye

hind leg

proboscis

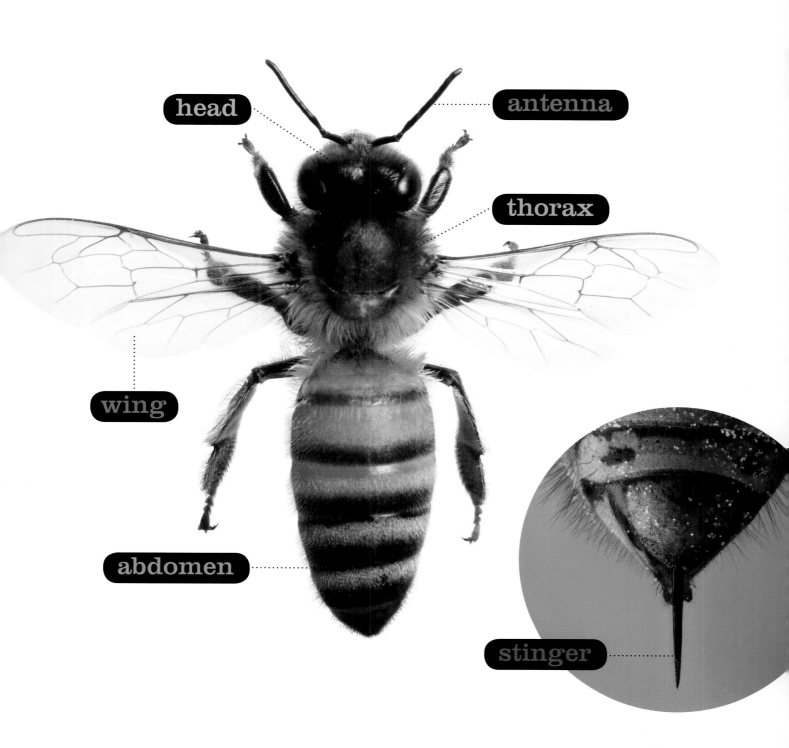

head

antenna

thorax

wing

abdomen

stinger

Words to Know

nectar: a sweet liquid that flowers make

pollen: a yellow powder that flowers make

stingers: pointy body parts that can sting

Read More

Allen, Judy. *Are You a Bee?*
New York: Kingfisher, 2001.

Sexton, Colleen. *Honey Bees.*
Minneapolis: Bellwether Media, 2007.

Websites

Bee Activities and Crafts
http://www.first-school.ws/theme/animals/insects/bee.htm
Choose a bee craft to do. Or print and color bee pictures.

Bee Facts for Kids
http://kids.sandiegozoo.org/animals/insects/bee
Learn more about bees from the San Diego Zoo.

Index